MW00387307

This book belongs to

_____

This book is dedicated to my children – Mikey, Kobe, and Jojo.
We all feel unmotivated sometimes and that's okay! Just know that you can
change it around if you want to.

Copyright © Grow Grit Press LLC. All rights reserved. No part of this book may be reproduced in any form
without permission in writing from the publisher. Please send bulk order requests to marynhin@gmail.com
978-1-951056-03-2 Printed and bound in the USA. First printing November 2019. GrowGrit.co

Lazy Ninja

Pictures by
Jelena Stupar

By Mary Nhin

On Friday morning, all of Lazy Ninja's friends were headed out to play dodgeball.

They asked Lazy Ninja to come, but he said, "No."

Instead...

Lazy Ninja stayed in his room
and played video games.

When everyone was headed to a slime fight and asked Lazy Ninja to join, he answered, "I don't think so."

Instead...

Lazy Ninja lounged on the couch eating Twinkies and binge-watched Netflix.

When his friends asked him to play soccer,
Lazy Ninja responded, "Nah."

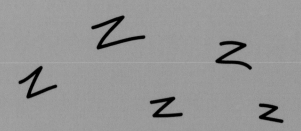

Lazy Ninja opted to stay on
the couch and nap.

That afternoon, his good friend, Inventor Ninja, came over and asked, "Do you want to know one of my tricks when I'm in a rut?"

I put on my tennis shoes and tie them up!

Lazy Ninja moaned and groaned but he, reluctantly, put on his shoes and tied them up.

Then, Inventor Ninja suggested they create something fun for Grumpy Ninja's birthday party that evening.

"This was fun to make," said Lazy Ninja.

After they were done, the Ninjas enjoyed a snack and talked about what they planned to do when they grew up.

It was time for Inventor Ninja to go but he promised to meet up with Lazy Ninja later at the party.

Afterwards, Lazy Ninja was getting ready to watch the next episode of Finn Farted when he remembered that the party started at 5pm.

And do know what he did next?

He put on his shoes.
Tied them up.
And headed to the party.

If you're ever feeling unmotivated, just put on your tennis shoes and tie them up. Doing this sets you into motion!

Sign up for new Ninja book releases at GrowGrit.co

[Instagram icon] @marynhin   @GrowGrit
#NinjaLifeHacks

[Facebook icon] Mary Nhin   Grow Grit

[YouTube icon] Grow Grit